Be[...]
Xm[...]
Pirri 2010

NORWICH
in the 1960s
Ten Years that Altered a City

PETE GOODRUM

AMBERLEY

For Richard, Beverley, Clive and Jane –
all of you born in 1960

Front cover photograph courtesy of Richard Thorne

First published 2013

Amberley Publishing
The Hill, Stroud
Gloucestershire, GL5 4EP

www.amberley-books.com

Copyright © Pete Goodrum, 2013

The right of Pete Goodrum to be identified as the Author
of this work has been asserted in accordance with the
Copyrights, Designs and Patents Act 1988.

All rights reserved. No part of this book may be reprinted
or reproduced or utilised in any form or by any electronic,
mechanical or other means, now known or hereafter invented,
including photocopying and recording, or in any information
storage or retrieval system, without the permission in writing
from the Publishers.

British Library Cataloguing in Publication Data.
A catalogue record for this book is available from the British Library.

ISBN 978 1 4456 1650 6 (print)
ISBN 978 1 4456 1669 8 (ebook)

Typeset in 10pt on 12pt Sabon.
Typesetting and Origination by Amberley Publishing.
Printed in the UK.

CONTENTS

ABOUT THE AUTHOR

Pete Goodrum is a Norwich man. He has had a successful career in advertising agencies, working on national and international campaigns, and now works as a freelance advertising writer and consultant.

Pete is also a successful author. His book *Norwich in the 1950s*, published by Amberley, topped the local bestseller charts for almost three months in 2012.

He also makes frequent appearances on BBC local radio covering topics ranging from advertising to music and social trends. A regular reader at live poetry sessions, and actively involved in the media, Pete has a real passion for the history of Norwich and Norfolk.

He lives in the centre of the city with his wife, Sue.

INTRODUCTION

The twentieth century was really getting into its stride by the end of the 1950s. The war would never be forgotten by those who had lived through it, but peace had brought change and progress. In Norwich, as in many towns and cities, much of the damage caused by bombing had been repaired by 1959. New buildings, a strong manufacturing sector and the arrival of independent television were all clear signals that Norwich had changed in the first complete decade of peace.

By the end of 1959, there were young people of almost working age who had no memory of the war. If you were born in 1945 you were a peacetime baby, and by the start of 1960 you were something entirely new. You were a teenager.

The next decade would see a new attitude from a new generation. All over the country, old attitudes and rules would be discarded. With peace and affluence came confidence and style.

In reality, nobody threw a master switch to turn the monochrome of 1950s Norwich into instant sizzling colour. It was more like a trickle charge that gradually seeped into the city and powered it up. It didn't change at midnight on 31 December 1959. But over the next ten years it altered a lot.

From the significant changes to the city centre, through the social and cultural revolution that defined the decade, to the events and developments that made the news, this is a look back at those ten years in Norwich: the 1960s. Ten years that altered a city.

Acknowledgements

As ever, I have many people to thank for their help in putting this book together. The ever-helpful Jonathan Plunkett has given me access to his father's photographs. George Plunkett's pictures of Norwich are a valuable insight into the city's history. Richard Thorne kindly gave me permission to use his photograph of the Haymarket. Paul Seaton at 3D and 6D Pictures Ltd was immensely helpful with pictures from the Woolworths' archives. Thanks to the University of East Anglia for permission to use shots from their collection. Special thanks to Rachel Lavender for her help. My friend Martin Eagle provided useful research material for which I'm grateful.

It was my good friend, Audrey Sharp, who was influential in my meeting Denagh Hacon, and my delivering a talk to the Norwich Group of the Norfolk Family History Society. It was there, in a remarkable and pleasing coincidence, that I met Jennie Polyblank. To discover that she was so closely linked to Norwich in the 1960s, and in particular the Gala, was both a great joy and the source of much help. Thank you Audrey, Denagh and Jennie.

On the same day I met Jennie I had also, in another remarkable coincidence, met Ian Clark of www.ianclarkmusic.com. An almost uncanny, and bordering on unhealthy, mutual fascination with Mods, Florsheim shoes and Bass Loafers took us into deep conversation, from which came Ian's kind permission to use some of his photographs, taken by his father. Thanks Ian.

Once again, I have to thank my father for his help in my research and allowing me to plunder his archives. Thanks Dad.

Thanks to Chris Lacey at Archant for permission to reproduce cuttings from *The Pink'un*.

My special thanks to Nicola Gale and the team at Amberley Publishing.

I have made every effort to track down and obtain permission for the use of all the material in this book, and have duly given credit. If there is anything in these pages that you believe belongs to you and I've not given credit, it is only because I couldn't find you. Some of the organisations featured have obviously long since disappeared. Please accept that I've used the material in good faith to help tell this story, and that I've done so with gratitude and respect.

And, of course, I have a huge debt of gratitude to my ever supportive wife, Sue. Without her help and patience, a project like this would simply not come to fruition. Thanks Susie.

1
AT THE CENTRE

Norwich city centre in the 1960s. New shops, ancient church, changing fashions. And kerbside parking. (*Photograph courtesy of Richard Thorne*)

A single picture can say so much about an entire decade. The photograph opposite takes in so many elements of the centre of Norwich during the 1960s. Dominating the background is the church of St Peter Mancroft. Already over 500 years old when this picture was taken, it looks down on the statue of Sir Thomas Browne, the great scholar, doctor and author who lived in Norwich from 1637 until his death in 1682.

These reminders of the city's antiquity are faced, from the other side of Haymarket, by architecture from a later time. The style of George Skipper is stamped into the decorative frontage of Skipper's Number 1, Haymarket, built in 1902. By the 1960s, the building was host to shops on the ground floor. It is the first building in Haymarket, and the Panks' shop in this picture is the first in the adjoining Orford Place. Panks were already long-established engineers, who had been diversifying since the 1950s when television and radio were becoming ever more popular. This city centre shop was part of their strategy to meet the 1960s demand for record players, radiograms and records.

Across the street is an even newer part of the city centre. Built on the site of the old Haymarket Cinema, Peter Robinson was shopping for the 1960s. A shiny new store selling the latest fashions, it was Norwich at its most modern. It was the Sheffield branch of Peter Robinson that would launch an in store department called Topshop. By 1970, it was a stand-alone brand, complete with its Topman spin off.

The ladies in this shot are not wearing the very latest styles, but are of a certain age and therefore perhaps rather resistant to the trends of the swinging decade. The man, however, is wearing a modern, 1960s suit. The cars are of the time, but despite an increase in car ownership and traffic it appears that it was still possible to park, at least a moped, at the kerbside.

Ancient and modern, side by side. Norwich was altering.

There is no better place to start the story of Norwich in the 1960s than in the city centre streets. From Davey Place, through London Street, up to St Stephens Street, Surrey Street, Westlegate and beyond, through the heart of the city.

These are the streets and thoroughfares that, as the 1960s got into gear, would alter. Along with much more.

Panks, 1962. The business was still operating from the 'iron shop' on Cattle Market Street as engineers. In the city centre, their shops were diversifying into the radios and TVs that 1960s Norwich wanted. (*Photograph by George Plunkett*)

Davey Place, June 1961. There was little sign of change in Davey Place by 1961. The shopfronts in this shot appear not to have embraced the impending retail revolution characterised by the likes of Peter Robinson. The shoppers are, however, free to walk, safe from traffic, although cycles were allowed. Just around the corner in London Street the concept of pedestrianised city centre streets would make more determined strides in 1960s Norwich, setting the pace for the country. (*Photograph by George Plunkett*)

Above: London Street, *c.* 1968. London Street has more than once been blighted by fire. In 1970 Garlands, the flagship branch of Debenhams, burned down there. This earlier fire at the Hector Powe tailoring shop meant that fire engines had to get into the pedestrianised street.

Access for such emergencies had been built into the plan for pedestrian only streets, and the owner of this Austin A40 had plainly needed to take advantage of the situation. The fire engine would not have needed to travel far, as the fire station at this time was still operational in Bethel Street. (*Photograph courtesy of Ian Clark at www.ianclarkmusic.com*)

Opposite: London Street, 1967. London Street is an ancient thoroughfare, and has had several names, including, at one point, 'Cockey Lane'. By 1963, it featured in an extensive report on *Traffic in Towns*. Published by Her Majesty's Stationery Office, the survey covered a number of towns and cities. The overall finding, or proposal, as far as Norwich was concerned, was that the relentless increase in motor traffic would need to be controlled. Limiting access for vehicles was the only way forward if the ancient parts of the city were to be preserved for the future. London Street and The Walk were singled out as candidates for change. In 1967, London Street became the first street of its kind in the UK to be fully pedestrianised. (*Photograph by George Plunkett*)

Above: St Andrews Street, 1968. This street would rapidly become a very busy traffic zone. As the street patterns altered, the traffic congestion moved around the city. The following photograph was taken later in the same year. (*Photograph by George Plunkett*)

Opposite: St Andrews Street, 1968. If the newly pedestrianised areas were making life easier for shoppers and protecting the architecture from damage, traffic was still a problem elsewhere. Double yellow lines were already a feature, to stop kerbside parking, but this stream of traffic in both directions shows that the city had a developing problem. Already there were far more cars than cycles.

The Bullard's Anchor Brewery chimney was still standing at this point. The smell of brewing beer in Westwick Street was as much a part of Norwich life in the 1960s as the aroma of chocolate from the Caley's factory at Chapel Field.

The Bullard's brewery was still there, but what was missing from St Andrews Street by 1968 was the old library on the corner of Duke Street. The long-serving building had been demolished after the new library was built in 1961. (*Photograph courtesy of Ian Clark at www.ianclarkmusic.com*)

The new 'Central Library' under construction, 1961. The building of a new library was one of the major changes to the city centre in the 1960s. Work had begun in 1961 and the picture above shows the building in its very early stages. Replacing the library on the corner of St Andrews Street and Duke Street, this was to be an altogether different building, and one very much of its time.

Planned as early as 1956, the building was to stand on the site now occupied by The Forum. Known as the Central Library, it was designed by the then City Architect David Percival. Breathtakingly modern with lots of glass, a mezzanine floor and lecture theatre, it also contained a stark reminder of recent history. Helped by almost £35,000 raised by the 2nd Division of the United States Air Force, the library contained The American Memorial Room. The funds also facilitated the installation of a memorial fountain in the library's courtyard. It contained stones from every state in the USA and, like the Memorial Room, commemorated the airmen of the 2nd Division who had died in action while stationed in Norfolk during the war. (*Photograph by George Plunkett*)

The Central Library appears on the Norwich skyline, 1962. Completed, the new library building soon established itself in the Norwich skyline, standing taller than the main section of City Hall. Officially opened by the Queen Mother in 1963, the Central Library was to have a tragically short life. On 1 August 1994, fire broke out in the building. It threatened the Norfolk Records Office housed in the basement and destroyed not only the building's future but also over 150,000 books, and much of what was held in the American Memorial Room. (*Photograph by George Plunkett*)

Work begins on extending the Bethel Street Police Station, 1966. This central area of the city was changing at a pace. Just three years after the library was opened, another project was underway, almost next door to it. In Bethel Street, the police station was being extended. (*Photograph by George Plunkett*)

Farm machinery on sale at cattle market on Castle Hill, 1960. (*Photograph by George Plunkett*)

However, it was another 1960s building project out beyond the ring road that would have a truly profound effect on this central area of the city. For centuries there had been a cattle market on Castle Hill, where the agricultural business of the county gathered every Saturday. By the 1960s, it was becoming impractical to have livestock herded through the increasingly busy streets every weekend.

As farming had progressed and developed, machinery sales had also become part of the market, spreading it further across Castle Hill. Many children of the 1960s enjoyed the spectacle, and have fond memories of being among the animals and farmers on a Saturday morning. It simply wasn't realistic, though, to believe that a weekly cattle market could continue in a modern city centre.

Discussions about moving the cattle market out of the city centre had begun before the war. During the 1930s, when the City Hall was under construction, there had been much debate about such projects, but nothing had come to fruition.

Cars parked at every kerbside and corner, animals in pens on the Castle Hill, and machinery sales spreading out into the streets as the market developed to meet modern agricultural needs; the old ways were proving almost impossible for a modern city centre.

Increasing pressure to reconsider the pre-war plans to move the cattle market out of the city was irresistible. City centre Saturdays in the 1960s needed to be about retail and shoppers. Cattle trading was no longer viable.

Eventually, construction of the new livestock market got under way. It opened at Harford in 1960, and heralded both the end of a tradition that dated back to the eighteenth century and the beginning of a new chapter in the agricultural history of Norfolk. It also altered weekend life in the centre of Norwich.

The new livestock market at Harford, 1960s. Custom-designed and built for purpose rather than fitting in to the city centre streets, the new livestock market rapidly established itself as an important part of Norwich, and Norfolk, life. (*Photographs by George Plunkett*)

All of the fun of the fair, 1965 style. Agricultural trading may have left the city centre in 1960, but the long-standing tradition of holding Bank Holiday fairs on the same site didn't. Immediately behind what was by then the new Anglia TV studios, the fair would be erected two or three times a year. With none of the breathtaking rides of the modern theme park, the good old funfair would arrive with its 'Big Wheel', 'Dodgems' and 'Wall of Death'. The darts stalls, and the plastic duck booths, the air rifle galleries and the swings would spread out across the less than level Castle Hill area. Flat-bed lorries cranked out power from their generators as music blared from primitive sound systems and the screams of the riders rang out. Many are the 1960s children of Norwich who have walked away from here proudly clutching a gold fish in a plastic bag as a prize. (*Photograph by George Plunkett*)

Just a few minutes away from Castle Hill, and beyond Tombland where the original Saxon market had stood in Norwich, Magdalen Street was as busy as ever. This area of the city would see huge amounts of alteration in the coming years. At the time this photograph was taken, there was ample evidence that concerns over traffic were justified.

Still standing in this early 1960s shot is the Mayfair Cinema. It had been the Cinema Palace before being renamed and refurbished in 1946. As the massive 1950s cinema audiences dwindled with the advent of television, the Mayfair was one of the early casualties. Closing in 1962, the site was, for a while, occupied by that very 1960s craze, a bowling alley. After that, and with supreme irony, it became a TV studio. That which had helped kill the Mayfair now stood in its place.

Magdalen Street, *c.* 1961. As the next two colour photographs show, heavy traffic was a two way affair in 1960s Magdalen Street. The street was destined for further, and equally dramatic, change. Part of the plan to address the traffic problem had been the construction of an 'inner ring road'. This was envisaged as a dual carriageway and seen as the means to carry traffic around, rather than through, the city centre.

It was to have a huge impact on Magdalen Street. The area was a maze of small streets, courtyards and alleyways, with Magdalen Street itself running straight thorough it and out to the city's edge. There had been a degree of improvement to the neighbourhood in the 1950s and now it was seen as somewhere with a vital role in 1960s improvements. The new dual carriageway would run across Magdalen Street on a flyover.

The project began with demolition and clearances, followed by the construction of the flyover. With it came the emergence of the Anglia Square development. The aftermath would remain controversial in Norwich for decades. (*Photograph courtesy of Ian Clark at www.ianclarkmusic.com*)

Magdalen Street, *c.* 1961. The impact of the 1960s on Magdalen Street was vast. If it was equalled anywhere it was in St Stephens Street. Then, as now, this was the street that motorists first encountered when approaching Norwich from the A11 or Newmarket Road. In 1961, it was already too narrow to deal with the traffic, and certainly unlikely to cope with projected increases in cars, buses and lorries coming in to the city. (*Photograph courtesy of Ian Clark at www.ianclarkmusic.com*)

St Stephens Street, 1961 and 1962. Perhaps it was a Sunday that accounts for the absence of traffic in the photograph above, but this shot of St Stephens in 1961 captures the street just before the widening programme that would dramatically alter it. Identified as an area for development in the 1945 *Plan for Norwich*, the street had already undergone some changes during the 1950s. In 1961 it had not, however, changed greatly. Nevertheless, within a year work had begun and the picture below, from 1962, shows the rapid development. (*Above: Photograph by George Plunkett*)

St Stephens Street, 1960s. Appropriately, these two views of St Stephens Street are in colour; it's as if the 1960s are arriving! The street was still narrow at the top but the new, wider pavement had arrived at the city end.

Much of the work was directly linked to the expansion of the Norwich Union offices. Not yet rebranded as Aviva, the insurance giant was a major player in the city's development, and their influence on the city is a recurrent theme throughout many decades.

The view looking towards Curls (now Debenhams) is redolent of the era with the then familiar, bright red Eastern Counties buses making their way through the city centre. (*Photographs courtesty of Ian Clark at www.ianclarkmusic.com*)

Surrey Street Bus Station, 1962. Central to most of the Eastern Counties bus routes was the bus station in Surrey Street. The Norwich Union offices already dominated Surrey Street by this time, and this view through the bus station clearly shows the new look Norwich establishing itself in the 1960s. (*Photographs by George Plunkett*)

Denmark Opening, 1960. The ubiquitous red buses were still relative newcomers. The Eastern Counties Omnibus Company had bought the old tram system in 1933 and it was then that they started to close it down and replace trams with motor buses. By 1935, the last tram route, from Newmarket Road to Cavalry Barracks, had closed. While Norwich city centre and its transport system was modernising, this elderly tram car, predecessor to the buses, was languishing in Denmark Opening.

The Great Eastern, 1961. The Great Eastern, on the corner of Queens Road and St Stephens Street. To all appearances in 1961 it was a permanent part of Norwich, but this main entrance to the city from the A11 and the south was only months away from major upheaval. (*Photograph by George Plunkett*)

The Kosy Korner Kafe, 1963. At the top of St Stephens Street, across the road from The Great Eastern, on the corner of Queens Road, The Kosy Korner Kafe was still open in 1963. This busy junction was about to change beyond recognition. (*Photograph by George Plunkett*)

The corner of Queens Road, 1964. The Kosy Korner Kafe had gone. Work was now in full swing to change the St Stephens junction. Bravely pointing out that it was 'Business as Usual', companies carried on as the construction of the new roundabout was started.

Traffic was a serious issue and Norwich was meeting the need to cater for the constant increase in cars and motor vehicles. It seemed to happen very quickly. Within months, the St Stephens and Queens Road junction was taking on a new identity. It started to look like the 1960s.

Car parking was now a serious issue, and in keeping with both the need for more spaces and the architectural trends of the day, the next car park would be a modern 'multi-storey' building.

The city was now altering at a considerable pace and there is a marked contrast between the era of The Kosy Korner Kafe and the big, modern junction and car park that would now greet people arriving in Norwich. (*Photograph by George Plunkett*)

Queens Road Car Park under construction, 1963. Now there was to be a new car park, and it was multi-storey. Hard against the ancient city walls, the new building highlights the modern era arriving in an ancient city. As is so often the case with pictures of this vintage, the absence of hard hats and safety equipment is an equally stark contrast with today's practices.

As the new car park and the work around it continued to change the city's skyline, there were other changes to come that would eventually be less visible. There was work to be done underground as well. (*Photograph by George Plunkett*)

The start of the St Stephens Subway, 1964. Even more innovatively, Norwich was to have a pedestrian subway under the busy new St Stephens and Queens Road junction.

In 1964, work began to excavate the underpass that criss-crosses beneath street level, allowing pedestrians to access St Stephens Street, Queens Road, Chapel Field Road and St Stephens Road.

The photograph shows the early stages of the work. In the background there is more evidence of modernisation. Key Markets had opened their supermarket in the newly refurbished St Stephens Street, a real sign of 1960s retailing.

In recent years, fears have been expressed that in the rush to modernise the area these diggings could have resulted in the loss of historical data. Similar fears had arisen during the work at Magdalen Street, when the flyover was constructed. Certainly, the foundations of the ancient city walls were a worry. Such was one of the costs of progress.

These huge changes to such a vital street and road junction in Norwich are a clear indication of how much the city was altered in the early 1960s. So much of what had been proposed in the 1945 *Plan for Norwich* had been delayed or discarded. The work of post-war repair had taken time and effort to put things back in order before building for a future could sensibly be addressed.

Now it was the 1960s. Things were starting to happen. In all walks of life there were profound changes taking place. This was a new era, and an altered Norwich was emerging to meet it.

If roundabouts and subways were a sign of the sixties, it was a change to the skyline that would perhaps be the most visible and potent symbol of the new decade. The construction of what by local standards was a 'skyscraper' in Westlegate was a bold move. Again, its standing next to ancient buildings heightened the modernity of the building, and gave some a cause for concern. (*Photograph by George Plunkett*)

Westlegate House under construction, April 1961. Architecturally, the building was interesting, with heraldic crests decorating the outside; somehow ancient heraldry didn't seem incongruous. It was the sixties. Anything could work. Sadly, by the twenty-first century the building had become an unoccupied eyesore. By 2013, plans were in place to restore it. (*Photograph by George Plunkett*)

Work had in fact begun on Westlegate House in 1959, but it is undoubtedly a part of the 1960s. With offices on its upper floors, it was a quintessentially modern place to work. But it was the coffee bar and restaurant on the ground floor that was to become such an integral part of the 1960s scene.

Trading for some of the time as 'Purdy's', the place oozed sixties style. Shiny and new, plastic and glass, it inevitably attracted the 'Mods'. Often, dozens of Vespa and Lambretta scooters would be parked at the kerb outside this slick establishment as the fashionable young people of Norwich called in to sip their coffee.

Norwich Union buildings, All Saints Green, 1962. Aviva was still known as Norwich Union in the 1960s. It's impossible to look at the history of the city at any time in the twentieth century without mentioning the company. St Stephens Street had been altered dramatically as they had expanded their offices in the 1960s. (*Photograph by George Plunkett*)

Norwich Union buildings, All Saints Green, 1962. These views are on All Saints Green, just around the corner from Surrey Street and the bus station. The buildings have their backs to St Stephens Street. George Skipper's 'Marble Hall' headquarters for the company, built in Surrey Street in 1905, defined their time. In 1962, these Norwich Union buildings were statements of their own new era. (*Photograph by George Plunkett*)

Gentleman's Walk, *c.* 1966. Even by the mid-1960s, not every street in Norwich was boasting as much progress, or seeing as much alteration, as St Stephens Street or Magdalen Street. Gentleman's Walk, for example, was still open to traffic. Opposite the Royal Arcade, the outer edges of the market place were occupied predominantly by fish stalls.

The empty premises at the top of The Arcade in this shot lend a slightly downbeat atmosphere to what in reality was a busy street. It would be revamped and enlivened further by becoming another pedestrian only zone. (*Photograph courtesy of Ian Clark at www.ianclarkmusic.com*)

Above: St Giles Street, 1962. St Giles Street, nestling behind the City Hall and running down to the Guildhall, is one of the city's older streets. In 1962, although changes were looming, the buildings were still a reflection of the old city, rather than the new. It was here, however, that the old Hippodrome would close and give way to a car park in another move to deal with the changing needs of the city. (*Photograph by George Plunkett*)

Opposite: Charing Cross, 1961. Charing Cross was another area that had altered very little in the decades leading up to the 1960s. In many of these glimpses into the 1960s, it is noticeable that the cars, like the big Ford parked here, were American-influenced designs that had arrived in the UK during the late 1950s. These 'modern' cars tend to create a stark contrast with the older, unaltered buildings, and emphasise the constantly growing love affair with the motor vehicle.

Around the corner from this scene, the streets had already seen some modernisation with the arrival of Norfolk House in St John Maddermarket. The numerous sites of development among the older buildings served to underline the point that Norwich was, out of necessity, altering, but that conservation was a key consideration. (*Photograph by George Plunkett*)

St Giles Street, 1962. Even the increase in traffic had not removed the luxury of parking at the kerbside and popping into a shop in 1962 St Giles Street. Lacey and Lincoln's ironmongery business was based in the fine terrace of buildings that would soon stand facing a brand new multi-storey car park. It would be built on the site of the much-loved, but no longer viable, Hippodrome.(*Photograph by George Plunkett*)

Grapes Hill, 1964. Along from St Giles Street is the top of Grapes Hill. This was another area to witness change in the 1960s. In 1964, Grapes Hill was still a narrow street of Victorian houses. Most of them would disappear as the new inner link road was developed and Grapes Hill became a dual carriageway. (*Photographs by George Plunkett*)

King Street, 1961. If further evidence were needed of the way in which Norwich altered at a variable pace, it is in areas like King Street and Theatre Street. These city centre locations are close to so much of the early 1960s upheaval and yet somehow, initially, seemed to get left behind. There were no shops in either of these streets, so they were not constantly crowded by pedestrians. Traffic was a reducing problem as the increasingly aware motorists knew better ways through the city. King Street had undergone slum clearance operations in the 1930s. During the war it was heavily bombed. Then, suddenly, the 1960s caught up with King Street. As the new Rouen Road was built, much of the old street was demolished. (*Photograph by George Plunkett*)

Theatre Street, 1962, Plunkett. In Theatre Street, home to the Assembly Rooms, nothing much had changed by 1962. Within a decade it would be altered considerably. (*Photograph by George Plunkett*)

Prince of Wales Road has always had importance, leading as it does straight to the railway station.

The passing decades have seen the road evolve, always embracing professional offices, places to eat and drink as well as shops.

At the bottom end, approaching the railway station, Prince of Wales Road looked a different place in 1964. Several well-known Norwich businesses, including Valoris, Lamberts and Major Mace, were trading in this now demolished run of shops. It is another part of the city where life seemed to have stood still at the start of the 1960s, before dramatic change altered the area completely. The newer street lamps had arrived in 1964, but it was still a time when cigarette machines could be found outside shops. It is a long way from the banks, supermarkets and offices that stand on this site today; and even further from the twenty-first-century nightlife that dominates Prince of Wales Road after dark.

Prince of Wales Road, towards the railway station, 1964. (*Photograph by George Plunkett*)

Prince of Wales Road, *c.* 1967. At the top end of Prince of Wales Road, just a few years later, it's a busier scene. New building work is in progress next to what was still a Norwich Union office. A look at this same spot, at the same time of day, in 1957 would reveal far more cycles and not so many cars. (*Photograph courtesy of Ian Clark at www.ianclarkmusic.com*)

2

IN THE NEWS

The concept of a university in the city had been discussed before and in the nineteenth century it was given serious consideration. It would take the post-war world to realise that it was time to do something. The 'baby boom' had produced a bigger population, and more of them had the chance to experience higher education. New universities were now a timely idea, and the news was that Norwich was an ideal location for just such an institution.

In 1962, the commission to design the University of East (UEA) Anglia went to a forty-eight-year-old London-based architect called Denys Lansdun. His track record included university buildings at Leicester, Liverpool and Cambridge. He had also designed blocks of flats in London and, before they opened in Norwich, the London store for Peter Robinson in The Strand. He'd also designed the National Theatre.

What was interesting about the commission for the UEA was that here was a chance to design and build a complete campus from scratch. This would be a unified whole from the start.

Lansdun's ideas were rooted in his admiration for Le Corbusier, and his design for the UEA was based on the use of concrete. It was going to be a thoroughly modern university in an extremely ancient city. Once again, the contrasts between old and new would leap into focus. Such was the stance of the university that the motto it adopted was 'Do Different'. The words are a clear indication that teaching, learning and academic achievement would be attained through a new vision for university life. They are also deeply connected to the arguably less academic, but equally determined, old Norfolk attitude.

The first students arrived at the University of East Anglia in 1963. By 1967, the famous 'Ziggurats' terraced student residences were complete. Also designed by Lansdun, these award-winning buildings were listed at number eight in the *Architects Journal* 'Top Ten' of UK university architecture.

The university itself is now world class, and consistently sought after by undergraduates. While the first students settled in to life at the new university, they were unaware that Norwich was the subject of a bizarre experiment. The story was not actually in the news in 1963 and 1964 because it was a secret, only coming to light in 2000. Rumours had circulated before this date, but almost forty years after the event the truth was out. Norwich had been sprayed with chemicals to test how a cloud would disperse biological agents. More than once, at night, the city had been sprayed with zinc cadmium sulphide.

The tests were very much part of the 'Cold War' mentality. The UK was seen as vulnerable and open to the devastation of a biological attack or chemical warfare. Scientists wanted to know how quickly a 'poison cloud' could spread, and how it would disperse.

There have been claims that cancer cases have risen as the direct result of the experiment, and suggestions that the tests may have caused respiratory diseases. The full truth may never be known. What is certain is that in 1963 and 1964, the people of Norwich did not know they were made the unwitting subjects of a test.

The new University of East Anglia square, 1960s architecture for a new campus. (*Photograph courtesy of University of East Anglia*)

Students at the University of East Anglia village in the 1960s. (*Photograph courtesy of University of East Anglia*)

St Augustine's swimming pool, 1962. (*Photography by George Plunkett*)

Norwich was ill-served for swimming pools until the 1960s. Lakenham Pool was a stalwart, and loved by generations of Norwich swimmers. Many Norwich residents will also remember learning to swim in the city's rivers at places such as the Dolphin Bridge on the Wensum, or in the fenced-off stretch of river in Wensum Park. Then came the big, new 1960s, and with them a new swimming pool. Designed by City Architect David Percival, the pool opened in March 1961. It was modern, clean and well equipped. Local clubs like the Swans, and Penguins, instantly used it. Schools took children there to learn to swim.

For many Norwich youngsters, this was the first time they'd experienced that smell of chlorine and the echoing noise of a brand new, custom-built swimming pool. Just as that other 1960s arrival, the new Central Library, has already gone, so too the St Augustine's swimming pool has served its purpose and already disappeared from Norwich life. Just over thirty years after it opened, the pool was closed in December 1996, and soon after that demolished. Norwich was, once again, without a municipal pool.

The YMCA had played a role in Norwich life since the nineteenth century. As early as 1856 there had been Nonconformist groups attempting to start such an organisation, with the aim of improving and enhancing the religious and moral lives of the younger male citizens.

Colman money helped with the acquisition of property in St Giles Street in the 1880s. During the war, in 1941, another hostel was opened in Bethel Street. In 1961 a recreation hall was constructed in Bethel Street.

YMCA recreation hall, Bethel Street, 1962. Norwich YMCA earned another place in history in 1969. Newly-weds Mr and Mrs Chandler became the first couple to spend their honeymoon there. (*Photograph by George Plunkett*)

For newly-married couples, and everyone else, post-war Norwich had a patchwork of housing. Gaps left by bombing had been built on in some places, but other empty spaces remained unused for years. Many families needed rehousing, either because of bomb damage, or as part of the slum clearance programmes. Many such families were housed in 'prefabs'.

Ketts Hill 'Prefabs', still in service in 1962 (*Photograph by George Plunkett*)

1960s housing arrives, Alderson Place off Queen's Road, 1962. (*Photograph by George Plunkett*)

The swimming pool and the library were planned as buildings for the future. Both had come and gone quite quickly. Ironically, the 'prefabs' were conceived as temporary structures but lasted longer than intended or expected.

The first 'prefab', or pre-fabricated house, was erected like a kit in 1946. It was part of the council's plan to provide temporary accommodation for families while the grand scheme to build 2,000 houses in five years got under way. It was vital work. Some 2,000 houses had been destroyed by enemy action and another 30,000 badly damaged.

There were 350 'prefabs' erected in Norwich, and they were designed to last for ten years. Many of them were still in service throughout the 1960s. In fact, the last one to be occupied was not dismantled until 1976.

Much more in the news in the 1960s was the progress in new council housing. As many of the old terraces disappeared, a new, more modern, residential style began to emerge. It was in step with the city centre developments and added to the emerging modernity of 1960s Norwich.

Midland Street, early 1960s. These houses and flats in Midland Street are typical of the 1960s buildings that replaced the old, Victorian streets.

This area of the city had been a warren of terraced streets, which by the 1960s were not up to the standards of modern living. The full programme of clearance took time, and it wasn't until the early 1970s that all those scheduled for demolition had been knocked down. In many areas the houses were modernised, becoming the fashionable small house of later years. (*Photograph by George Plunkett*)

Eastern FOOTBALL NEWS

(THE PINK UN)

Telephone 28311

Telegrams "Press." Norwic

No. 1522—Fourpence

Saturday, February 18, 1967

and   3   Cup

ON THE BALL

A T A S H A

Canaries' great triumph at Old Trafford

CHESTER UTD. ... 1   NORWICH CITY 2

VE DONE IT! And there'll be high jinks in Norwich
onight. The Canaries, unranked and the biggest of big
s, whipped the F.A. Cup favourites, Manchester United,
Trafford today in the biggest Cup upset for years.

golden goals — indeed, two golden gift goals — rattled United's
Goals by Don Heath and Gordon Bolland put the Canaries on
t of their biggest wave since 1959. The match closed in
led scenes of jubilation and despair. Yellow-and-green-bedecked
supporters worked themselves into ecstasy in their side's magnifi-
ay.

ter United — Stepney; Dunne,
erand Sadler, Stiles, Ryan,
ton, Herd, Best. Sub., Aston.

City — Keelan; Stringer,
cas, Brown, Allcock, Kenning.
ryceland, Bolland, Anderson.
k.

—W. J. Gow (Swansea).
llcock and the Canaries were
o the pitch by the Dagenham

By
DICK SCALES

Stiles covered Dunne well and pre-
vented Anderson from breaking
through

KEVIN KEELAN

EVERY

When it comes to sport in Norwich in the 1960s, it is of course to Norwich City that most memories return. It was always going to be difficult for the Canaries to recoup the glory of their wonderful 1959 cup run, but the fans were there to cheer the team into the new decade.

It began well. In the 1959/60 season, Norwich were promoted to the Second Division after coming second to Southampton. The 1960/61 season saw them finish well, although there was a brush with glory when Ron Ashman guided them to defeat Rochdale 4-0 in a two-leg final to win the win the League Cup.

Promotion to the First Divison escaped them in the 1960s, with sixth place being their highest achievement.

Two occasions stand out in the club's 1960s era. Although knocked out by Leicester in the sixth round of the cup, in 1963 they once more demonstrated the incredible support they could engender in their fans. On that fateful day, Saturday 30 March 1963, they may have lost 2-0, but a record-breaking 44,000 people crammed in to Carrow Road to see their heroes, and share the agony.

1967 would see another example of Norwich City's giant killer attitude. As had been the case before, the Canaries were rank outsiders when they took on the legendary Manchester United in a cup game on 18 February 1967. The Manchester team included stellar names such as Charlton, Law, Best and Stiles. There was a crowd of over 63,000. It looked like a foregone conclusion.

But ninety minutes later even the United players were applauding the City players off the field. In one of the most dramatic cup upsets ever, Norwich City were 2-1 winners.

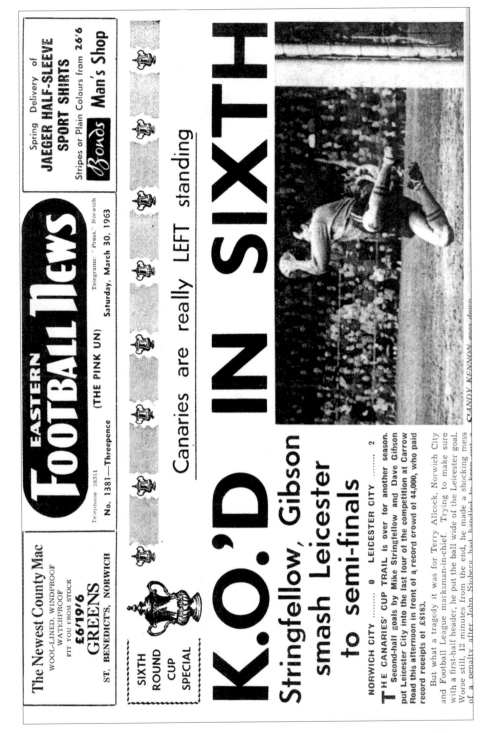

The Newest County Mac

WOOL-LINED, WINDPROOF
WATERPROOF

FIT YOU FROM STOCK

£6/19/6

GREENS

ST. BENEDICT'S, NORWICH

Spring Delivery of

JAEGER HALF-SLEEVE
SPORT SHIRTS

Stripes or Plain Colours from 26/6

Bonds Man's Shop

EASTERN FOOTBALL NEWS

(THE PINK UN)

Telephone 28311   Telegrams: "Press," Norwich

No. 1381—Threepence   Saturday, March 30, 1963

Canaries are really LEFT standing

K.O.'D IN SIXTH

SIXTH
ROUND
CUP
SPECIAL

Stringfellow, Gibson smash Leicester to semi-finals

NORWICH CITY 0   LEICESTER CITY 2

THE CANARIES' CUP TRAIL is over for another season. Second-half goals by Mike Stringfellow and Dave Gibson put Leicester City into the last four of the competition at Carrow Road this afternoon in front of a record crowd of 44,000, who paid record receipts of £8183.

But what a tragedy it was for Terry Allcock, Norwich City and Football League marksman-in-chief. Trying to make sure with a first-half header, he put the ball wide of the Leicester goal. Worse still, 12 minutes from the end, he made a shocking mess of a penalty after John Sjoberg had handled to keep out a

CANDY KENNON goes down

The Pink'un, 30 March 1963. Actually printed on white paper at this stage, the famous *Eastern Football News* records the sad defeat but joyously huge crowd.

Chadds BEDFORD STREET NORWICH

TWO - PIECE SUITS

from **13 gns.** to **25 gns.**

Sizes from 34 to 46

MOVEMENT AFOOT

The Man's Shoe Department has now moved to the Man's Shop

LOWER GROUND FLOOR

Bonds **MAN'S SHOP**

EASTERN FOOTBALL News

(THE PINK UN)

Telephone 28511

No. 1522—Fourpence

Telegrams "Press." Norwich

Saturday, February 18, 1967

WHAT A SHAKER

Heath and Bolland K.O. the Cup favourites

Canaries' great triumph at Old Trafford

MANCHESTER UTD. ... 1   NORWICH CITY 2

WE'VE DONE IT! And there'll be high jinks in Norwich tonight. The Canaries, unranked and the biggest of big outsiders, whipped the F.A. Cup favourites, Manchester United, at Old Trafford today in the biggest Cup upset for years.

Two golden goals — indeed, two golden gift goals — rattled United's defence. Goals by Don Heath and Gordon Bolland put the Canaries on the crest of their biggest wave since 1959. The match closed in unparalleled scenes of jubilation and despair. Yellow-and-green-bedecked Canaries supporters worked themselves into ecstasy in their side's magnificent display.

Manchester United — Stepney; Dunne, Noble, Crerand, Sadler, Stiles, Ryan, Law, Charlton, Herd, Best. Sub, Aston.

Norwich City — Keelan; Stringer, Mullett, Lucas, Brown, Allcock, Kenning, Heath, Bryceland, Bolland, Anderson. Sub, Black.

By

DICK SCALES

KEVIN KEELAN flies between Denis Law and Terry Allcock

RESULTS AT A GLANCE

F.A. CUP—4th Rd.

Bolton	0	Arsenal	0-0
Brighton	1	Chelsea	0-1
Bristol C.	1	Soton	0-1
Cardiff	1	Man. C.	1-1
Fulham	1	Sheff. U.	0-0
Ipswich	2	Carlisle	0-0
Leeds	5	W. Brom.	4-0
Liverpool	1	Aston V.	1-0
Man. U.	1	Norwich	2-1
Nottm. F.	3	Newcastle	1-0
Roth'ham	0	B'ham	1-0
Sheff. W.	4	Mansfield	0-1
Sund'land	7	Peterboro'	4-0
Swindon	2	Bury	1-0
Tottenh'm	3	Ports'th	1-0
Wolves	1	Everton	1-0

DIVISION II

The Pink'un, 18 February 1967. A massive victory and cup tie upset.

The Speedway, 1963, twenty heats and dancing to the starbeats.

The other popular sport of the time was still Speedway. The motorcycle racing in Norwich had always been a big attraction and during the 1960s big crowds still gathered at the stadium on Holt Road to see star riders.

This advertisement for the Malcolm Flood Memorial Trophy from 1963 gives some indication of the sense of occasion that a night at the Speedway was.

DALE MARTIN PROMOTIONS LTD proudly present

WRESTLING!

THE CORN HALL
EXCHANGE STREET
NORWICH

SATURDAY, MARCH 30th

A Dale Martin 'Stars of TV' Tournament

Doors open 6.45 p.m.
Commence 7.30 p.m.

JOSEF ZARANOFF (Leningrad) v **GERRY DE JAGER** (Johannesburg)

TOOMA (West Africa) v **JEAN MORANDI** (France)

JEAN CORNE (Paris) v **CLIFF BEAUMONT** (Wigan)

KARL VON CHENOK v **REG TROOD** (Kensington)

Tickets and Advance Bookings obtainable from Geo Wortley Ltd., 4, Charing Cross, Norwich (Norwich 26254/5)   Prices 10/-, 7/6, 5/- and 3/6   Children Admitted to Standing at Half Price Only if Accompanied by Adult   All rights of admission strictly reserved

Meanwhile, for 'grappling fans' as the TV commentators called them, there was wrestling. A curious mixture of sport and theatre, the wrestling bouts had become steadily more popular thanks to regular Saturday afternoon TV coverage. It is often said that it was much loved by 'grannies', but some of the star wrestlers became household names in the 1960s.

In 1963, the wrestling matches were still held in the old Corn Hall on Exchange Street. By 1967, they had followed their 'agricultural connection' and moved to the new Livestock Market at Harford.

DALE MARTIN PROMOTIONS LTD.,

WRESTLING

NEW CATTLE MARKET

NEW CORN EXCHANGE, HALL ROAD, HARFORD

Doors Open 6.45 p.m.   **TONIGHT**   Commence 7.30 p.m.

AN INTERNATIONAL HEAVYWEIGHT CONTEST

TOGO TANI (Tokio, Japan) v **IRISH PAT BARRATT** (Dublin)

TONY COSTAS v **YOUNG ROBBY. BRIAN TREVORS** v **PASQUALE SALVO.**

JOHNNY YEARSLEY v **EZZARD HART**

Tickets and Advance Bookings from CEO WORTLEY LTD., 4 Charing Cross, Norwich, Norwich 26254/5. Prices 10/6, 8/-, 6/- and 4/-. Platforms for the convenience of standing patrons. Hall centrally heated   Unlimited car parking space.

4

UP TO DATE

The 1960s was a decade of restless social change. The streets of Norwich may not have been transformed overnight, and not all the immediately post-war, or indeed pre-war, values were immediately overturned, but the atmosphere was changing. There were new things to do, new clothes to wear and new places to go.

There was also a new reason to stay in. Television was becoming more popular and more accessible by the day. The Coronation of Elizabeth II in 1953 had been the turning point. Although public service television had been broadcast in Britain since 1936, it was the spectacle of a Royal occasion that had entranced the nation and propelled the medium from almost a gimmick into a way of life.

By the 1960s, television was the entertainment force to be reckoned with. It had grown beyond its original one BBC channel. There was independent TV as well. Anglia Television had been established in Norwich in 1959.

By the end of the 1960s there would be a third channel called BBC 2 and colour television had arrived. 200,000 homes had a colour set in 1969, a relatively tiny number, but by the mid-seventies almost every home had a 'colour telly'.

Even by today's standards, the output of the television companies was prolific and important. Some of the most legendary TV programmes ever made were produced in the 1960s. *Doctor Who, Coronation Street, The Avengers, Z Cars, Till Death Us Do Part*, and *The Likely Lads* all arrived on the nation's flickering screens in the 1960s. The audience and programme makers were totally unaware of their enduring appeal. Some of the new programmes were of their time; this was the era of satire and 'That Was The Week That Was'. It was a time of breaking rules and entering into uncharted waters. Watching and commenting was Mary Whitehouse, self-appointed guardian of 1960s morals.

Fighting a valiant, but ultimately futile, battle for supremacy was the cinema. In Norwich, as everywhere, once loved and regularly attended cinemas were falling victim to the box in the corner of the living room. Already mentioned, the Mayfair in Magdalen Street had closed its doors. One of the next 1960s victims in Norwich was the Theatre de Luxe.

Standing on St Andrews Street, the Theatre de Luxe had been the first cinema in Norwich, opening for business in 1910. The tragedy of the place, in relation to the story of the 1960s, is not just that it succumbed to changing tastes, but that it stood empty, like a spectre, for the whole of the decade. Closed for business as early as 1957, it wasn't demolished until 1970.

For ten years, the litter piled up in the outer foyer, behind the grilles that had once held back the queues until it was time for the next showing. The traffic thundered past in St Andrews Street and the once grand interior remained invisible.

The Theatre de Luxe, St Andrews Street, mid-1960s. At the very end of the decade, the interior was all too visible again. As the demolition got under way, what had once been the darkened auditorium was laid bare to the street and the sky. (*Photograph courtesy of Ian Clark at www.ianclarkmusic.com*)

Not all cinemas gave up and closed during the 1960s. Those that had geared themselves up for the decade not only survived but, for some key movie moments of the 1960s, had queues around the block like the old days. In a pre-Beatlemania world, Cliff Richard and the Shadows were Britain's coolest combo and when their movie *Summer Holiday* was released, the queues outside the ABC on Prince of Wales Road were enormous.

This was also the era of some of the early James Bond films and they meant big business too. *The Sound of Music, Lawrence of Arabia, Zulu* and many more were there to be seen at the Odeon, the Carlton, The ABC and the Gaumont.

Picture-going was still popular, but the glory days of the 1950s, when whole families went more than once a week, had gone. Now it was more of an event, and that fitted with the emerging trend for 'epics' and big production movies.

The fact was that if you were not of an age to go to see bands, or dance in the clubs and ballrooms, there was more home entertainment available than ever before. And Norwich retailers were there to meet the demand. Panks, Willmott's on Prince of Wales Road and the Televison Centre all had not just televisions, but tape recorders, radios, radiograms and record players to offer. And there was High Fidelity too.

For *TAPE RECORDERS . . .*
— *and HIGH FIDELITY*

★ QUAD · LEAK · PYE · ROGERS · GOODMANS

★ WHARFEDALE · FERROGRAPH · VORTEXION, etc

OUR HI-FI MANAGER, MR. J. D. DUGGAN, WILL BE PLEASED TO DEMONSTRATE EQUIPMENT & GIVE ADVICE ON SUITABLE SYSTEMS FOR YOUR LISTENING PLEASURE

Phone
28441

TELEVISION CENTRE
(TUMILTY ELECTRIC LTD.)
62-66 ST. GILES STREET · NORWICH

Phone
28441

★ ★ ★ ★ ★ EAST ANGLIA'S LEADING HIGH FIDELITY SPECIALISTS ★ ★ ★ ★ ★

Above: The Television Centre: 'East Anglia's Leading High Fidelity Specialists', 1960. Even though the equipment was improving, and the music scene was changing as the eruption of popular taste, spearheaded by The Beatles, drew closer, there was still a restrained atmosphere to the world of records and record players.

The Television Centre had obviously separated their TV sales approach from their music-lovers, but this advertisement, typical of its time, is not exactly 'rock and roll'.

Serious 'High Fidelity' at this point was for the classical music lover, or the modern jazz fan. Those still clinging to the world of Sinatra, who was producing impeccable albums that defined the era, would also appreciate the finer sounds of the stereo long player.

Opposite: The Theatre de Luxe, 1970. Demolition revealed the wonderful interior for the last time. (*Photograph courtesy of Ian Clark at www.ianclarkmusic.com*)

Your favourite Record!

will sound better on

"HIGH - FIDELITY"

Reproducing Equipment

We cordially invite you to visit our new "HI FI" Demonstration Room *at 62 St. Giles Street, Norwich, to see and hear the latest reproducing equipment by PERIOD—LEAK—WHARFEDALE—QUAD GOODMAN—PYE—ROGERS, etc.*

TELEVISION AND RECORD CENTRE

20 WENSUM STREET
(near Fye Bridge, Norwich,

62 ST. GILES STREET
(opp. St. Giles Church, Norwich)

(TUMILTY ELECTRIC LTD.)
Tel: Norwich 28441/2

*Confidential Hire Purchase Terms
Available*

MARKET PLACE
North Walsham Tel: 3260

MARKET PLACE, DISS
Tel: 2467

The Television and Record Centre, 1961, very politely explaining that they have more than TV. By 1962, if you were a teenager, it wasn't High Fidelity you wanted. Mono was fine, because a 7" single played on your tiny Dansette turntable was all you needed to make yourself happy and drive your parents crazy.

RECORD PLAYER
or
TRANSISTOR RADIO

Over 20 Models from which to choose.
Here are a few examples:

CAPRI Transistor Radio .... at 10½ gns.
POPULAR Non-Auto Player ... at 10 gns.
TEMPO Auto-Change Player ... at 15½ gns

Willmott's
WILLBRO HOUSE
45-51 PRINCE OF WALES RD. NORWICH
Tel. No. 23101   NOR 01S

TRANSISTOR RADIOGRAM
at 23 Gns.

Dansette: the teenage essential in 1963, and available at Wilmott's on Prince of Wales Road.

Norwich by the early 1960s did, however, have a healthy 'live' music scene. Most of the dance halls, including the Samson and Hercules, were still quite traditional in their approach, usually offering a house band for dancing. Pubs and coffee bars were catering for the folk music fans and the legendary Jolly Butchers, hosted by the equally legendary 'Black Anna', had become a haunt for those interested in the blues.

And then it happened. Possibly the most important gig in the history of Norwich. Other bands would play in the city, some of enormous importance, but on 17 May 1963, The Beatles arrived in Norwich.

Already famous with a single and an album in the charts, the group were on the threshold of greatness. When local promoter Ray Aldous booked them in April that year for £250, nobody, even then, could have foreseen the impact they were about to have on international culture. The group, which just a few years later would record *Sgt Pepper's Lonely Hearts Club Band*, be multi-millionaires and have a place in history as unquestionably the most important band in pop history, arrived in Norwich in a blue Bedford van.

The venue for their two twenty-minute sets was the Grosvenor Rooms on Prince of Wales Road. Their pre-performance relaxation was to go to the ABC cinema next door. Their after show entertainment was fish and chips in a Rose Lane chip shop.

1,700 people were in the Grosvenor that night. Warming them up for The Beatles was local band Ricky Lee and the Hucklebucks. This was no small challenge. How do you play to 1,700 people waiting for The Beatles? They carried it off in considerable style.

It was to be the only time that The Beatles played Norwich. Their fee for the night was £250. To see them, and Ricky Lee and The Hucklebucks, would cost you 7s 6d (37.5p). Interestingly for a Beatles concert, the evening included a buffet.

The Beatles changed the world in 1963, and Norwich was moving with the times. By the mid-1960s, pop music was a dominating force in the nation's life in a way that is almost unimaginable today. Fashion trends moved in parallel with music, and soon the Teddy Boys of the 1950s were out of date and left behind by the two emerging youth cults of the 1960s. This was a pre 'hippy' era. This was the time of Mods and Rockers.

The legacy of the Teddy Boys' obsession with rock and roll was passed to the Rockers. Leather-clad, motorcycle-riding and wearing their 'Brylcreemed' hair in a quiff not dissimilar to the Teds, the Rockers liked the cafés, such as the 3C's and the Number Ten in Norwich. They hung around the motorcycle shops and had few sartorial aspirations other than a black leather motorcycle jacket and jeans.

On the other side of the fashion fence were the Mods. These were the post-war working-class boys and girls who had discovered style – Italian and 'Ivy League' clothing, good shoes, styled hair and an obsession with the music coming out of American labels such as Tamla Motown, Stax and Atlantic. If the Rockers were still happy to rock to Jerry Lee Lewis, the Mods wanted to look good and groove to Otis Redding.

Rockers did not need new shops for their clothes. The motorcycle shops and the government surplus stores amply catered for their needs. The Mods, on the other hand, had to have the latest fashions. A trend could change in a heartbeat; what was cool last week could be a sartorial crime this week. Of all the shops that catered for this insatiable craving for clothes, one name stands above all others. Aside from very specialist retailers like John Stephens in London, and a certain tolerance of some of Austin Reed's ranges, only one, more or less national, retailer could deliver what the Mods wanted, and they had a shop in Norwich. Harry Fenton.

FRIDAY

MAY 17th

GROSVENOR

PRINCE OF WALES ROAD

FABULOUS ATTRACTION

Great Visit—TV Stars, etc.

It's a must for those who like to twist, jive, rave

They are entertainment themselves

"PLEASE, PLEASE ME"
"FROM ME TO YOU"

Who else could make such sensational recordings other than

THE
BEATLES

The group with the 1963 sound, etc.

Also

RICKY LEE

and the

HUCKLEBUCKS

Licensed Bar, Buffet, etc.

8-11. Admission: before 8.30, 7/6; after 8.30 8/-

Friday 17 May 1963. Popular beat combo The Beatles play Norwich, 'The group with the 1963 sound'.

With the possibly already slightly less than cool advertising line of 'He dresses the stars, why not you?', Harry Fenton had the Ben Sherman shirts, the Levi jeans and the three button jackets that said Mod.

These were not the Ben Sherman button-downs that would reappear in later years as part of the Skinhead, or even Mod revival movements. This was their first appearance for a fashion-obsessed group who were all but unprecedented. Baby Boomers with no memory of war, money in their pockets and an attitude that said we can have good quality clothes as much as the next man. It was a working-class stand for style.

Jackson the Tailor had a branch in Norwich too, and that was where the Mods went to be measured for the sharp, three-button, centre-vented suits. At 21 guineas they often cost more than a Mod's father earned in a week.

As for transport, a Mod needed to get around, look good and not get dirty. The answer was to pull an ex-USA Army Parka over your suit and ride an achingly cool, and obviously Italian, scooter.

The two tribes could not have looked more different.

When it came to where to go on your chosen mode of transport, the differing factions had equally disparate ideas. Occasionally, a band would appeal to both types and there would be tense moments for the management as Mods and Rockers arrived at the same place. But as the sixties moved on, it is fair to say that Rockers were less interested in dancing. The result was that the two biggest venues for live gigs became places that Mods went to pose.

In Oak Street, the old 'Industries Club' had shifted with the times. The slightly older regulars were replaced with a crowd who wanted to see the extraordinary array of talent booked to play there. In a less than impressive building, in a less than busy street, Norwich hosted The Small Faces, The Kinks, The Riot Squad, Cream, Jethro Tull and many more. Among local bands to play, there were The Precious Few who rushed to near stardom with their version of 'Young Girl'. Never to make the national big time, they were adored by the Norwich fans.

Meanwhile at the top of St Stephens, the other important venue was the Gala. The Gala Ballroom had been part of Norwich life for a long time. Like the Industries Club, it had catered for a previous era, and it had very much been part of the ballroom dancing years.

Harry Fenton, St Stephens, 1966. No self-respecting Mod would have missed Ben Sherman shirts at Harry Fenton. (*Photograph courtesy of Ian Clark at www.ianclarkmusic.com*)

St Stephens Street, 1962. In the era of St Stephens still looking as it did in the above picture, it took only a step into the Gala to find a touch of glamour. Built in the early 1950s by Fred Read, at a cost of £8,000, the ballroom had opened in 1954. The maple dance floor alone had cost £1,000 and on the opening night, the queue to test it out was so big that people had to be turned away. At that stage the music was provided by the Gala Quartet and the dancing was strictly ballroom. (*Photograph by George Plunkett*)

The Gala Ballroom. A touch of 1950s glamour. The ballroom was extended in 1959 and is seen here in all its splendour. The 1960s were about to arrive. (*Photograph courtesy of Jennie Polybank*)

Indeed, the Gala was inextricably linked to dancing. It was to be the home of the Eileen Page School of Dancing, run by Laurie Singer and his wife, Eileen Page.

Eileen and Laurie ran the hugely successful dance school at the Gala for years. In the late 1950s and early, pre-Beatle 1960s, ballroom dancing was a useful social skill. Dancing Schools like Eileen Page, and the Norman School of Dancing were the places to learn, and meet members of the opposite sex.

The Eileen Page school's advertising of the period captures the times and clearly shows how important it was to learn to dance.

Eileen and her husband Laurie left Norwich in the mid-1960s. By then the tempo, and volume, of music in the Gala was changing. Just like the club in Oak Street, the Gala began to book top bands of the day; with them came the fans. Mainly, but not exclusively, Mod the crowds jammed the Gala to see the acts that were dominating the charts. Popular from the day it opened, the Gala was now an essential weekend venue.

The Eileen Page School of Dancing. What young lady could resist this advertising? This was the sure fire way to social success, and possibly romance. (*Courtesy of Jennie Polyblank*)

The Gala Ballroom, late 1960s. (*Photograph courtesy of Ian Clark at www.ianclarkmusic.com*)

Still one of '*the* places to go', the Gala was having to change again by the late 1960s. The posters in the picture above say it all. There was now a discothèque. Dancing to records was not new, but it had grown steadily during the 1960s, coming originally from the cellar clubs in 1960s Paris. Having little to do with its later, derivative disco craze, it was a way to get in the crowds without the cost of a band. The Gala's discothèque was offering Motown, Reggae and Pop, giving an interesting insight into both the current music trends and the varied audience they attracted. Motown and Reggae would have been acceptable to the still prevalent Mods. They would have considered pop too 'commercial'

Dancing to live acts was also still possible on Saturday nights, but the posters coyly refer to 'Guest Groups' rather than promise specific acts. The reference to DJs on dance night was by now not a request to wear dinner jackets. This was the time of disc jockeys playing record sets between the sessions by live bands. And it was simply playing records. The DJs of 1968 bore little resemblance to the high-tech shows of today's star performers. A light show sequenced to the beat was about as sophisticated as it got, even for the Gala.

But, another trend had emerged and had become almost a commercial necessity for some venues to stay in profit. Bingo! Loved by those of a certain age, it was seen as the death knell of society by intellectuals, and considered boring by teenagers.

Among the Norwich venues that would never have offered bingo was the seriously cool in attitude, but hot in temperature, Orford Cellar. Apart from putting on less than 'commercial' but very hip bands, including the Long John Baldry outfit that featured the young Rod 'the Mod' Stewart, the Orford is etched into the history of Norwich in the 1960s for two very important reasons. Firstly, it was the setting for some tremendous performances by Geno Washington and the Ram Jam Band. Washington was an American, stationed in the UK with the United States Air Force. He had often stood in for other singers in bands and it was in a London club that guitarist Pete Gage heard him and asked him to join his Ram Jam Band. It would become Geno Washington and the Ram Jam Band. A phenomenal live act, pumping out high voltage soul, the band did not translate to recording, except, that is, for live recordings. Their first album, *Hand Clappin, Foot Stompin, Funky-Butt, Live!,* captured the atmosphere of their gigs. It was both a cult classic and a commercial success. In 1966, it spent thirty-eight weeks on the charts, only to be outsold only by *The Sound of Music* and the massive *Bridge Over Troubled Water* by Simon and Garfunkel.

There were more records to come, but it was on stage that the band was at its best. Washington, a mercurial performer, became a cult figure in soul and R & B circles. Pete Gage went on to work with Elkie Brooks, before marrying her and joining with her and Robert Palmer to form Vinegar Joe.

Where they all went is not the issue. The point is that if you were a teenage Mod in the Orford Cellar on one of the nights Geno Washington and the Ram Jam Band played, or if you were at their St Andrew's Hall concert, you were present at a wildly exciting moment in 1960s Norwich.

If Geno Washington slipped from massive success, the other great name to play at the Orford sadly slipped, too early, from life itself. Nobody could have known that he had only three years to live when the unfeasibly talented Jimi Hendrix played at the Orford in January 1967. Within those three years, he would be catapulted to super-stardom, acknowledged as perhaps the greatest guitarist in rock history and die at the age of twenty-seven. Once the highest paid artist in the world, with defining performances at Woodstock and Monterey, he would die in sketchy and wretched circumstances in London. Those present at the Orford that night in 1967 were witnessing a genius in performance. Reports claim that backstage he was a shy man. On stage he stormed the place.

There were, of course, other places to go in 1960s Norwich. The Samson and Hercules ballroom on Tombland was still open. Popular with American troops during the war and reinvented as a nightclub in the 1990s, it had also been the original home of the Norman School of Dancing. In the 1960s, it was a busy, if slightly traditional, dancehall. There was also dancing at the Norwood Rooms, which was a rather more formal venue.

This was a pivotal point in social history. Wimpy Bars and Golden Egg cafés had arrived to cheer up the high street, but the explosion of steak houses and restaurants that would define the 1970s had not yet arrived. Ballroom dancing was on the wane, but if you were 'grown up', the dinner-dance was a sophisticated Saturday night's entertainment. And of course there was the television, and bingo.

The truth is that it was the time of the teenager. To be where the most fun, the coolest music and the fashions of the moment were, you needed to be young.

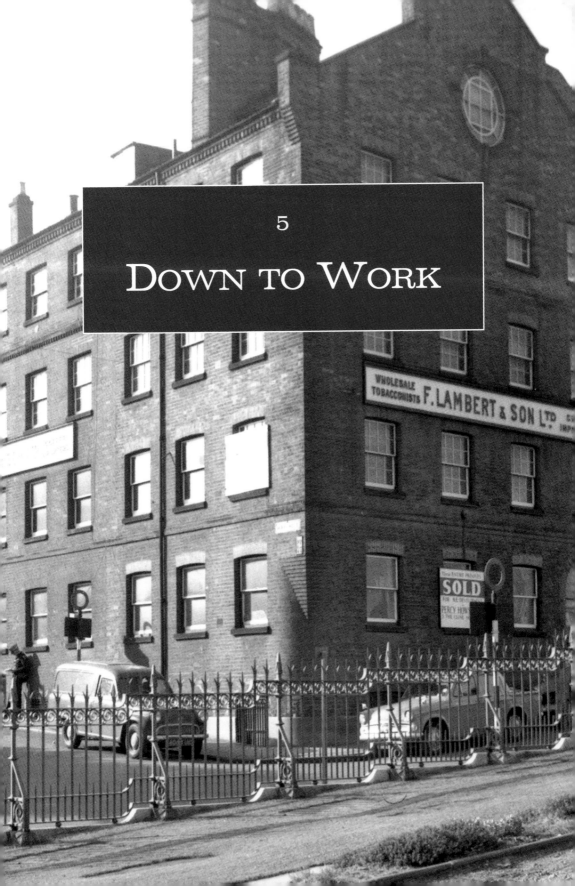

5

DOWN TO WORK

Above: Woolworths, Rampant Horse Street, 1968. 'Woolies' had been an essential part of the British high street for decades, and it met the 1960s boom times head on with modernisation plans for flagship branches like the Norwich Rampant Horse Street store. (*Photograph courtesy of 3D and 6D Pictures Limited*)

Opposite: Boston's, Norwich, 1960s. The 1960s were certainly a time of change, but for some businesses it was just another decade in a long history. Boston's, for example, near the Castle, had been retailing in Norwich since the 1850s.

The big Norwich names, companies like Norwich Union, Caleys and Colmans, were still important employers. Shoemaking was still a major part of the city's economy and workforce.

Times were easier compared to the rationing and shortages of the immediate post-war period, and that meant opportunities in retail. The Norwich branch of Woolworths rose to the challenge. It took a while, but by 1968 their Rampant Horse store had been modernised and extended. (*Photograph courtesy of Ian Clark at www.ianclarkmusic.com*)

Page 71: Lamberts Warehouse, 1966. (*Photograph by George Plunkett*)

Above: Woolworths food hall, Rampant Horse Street, 1968. The brand new 'serve-yourself' food hall at Woolworths had embraced the new supermarket style of shopping. It is easy to forget how new a concept this was in the 1960s. There was more choice than many people could ever remember having, and you simply wandered around at your own pace to pick and choose as you wanted. It was consumer heaven, a treat for those old enough to remember the bad times, and a statement by the younger generation to say 'this is modern, this is how it will be from now on'. (*Photograph courtesy of 3D and 6D Pictures Limited*)

Left: Woolworths, the new escalators, Rampant Horse Street, 1968. Not the first escalators in Norwich, but still an impressive feature in the 1960s.

Below: Woolworths, the new restaurant, Rampant Horse Street, 1968. Located on the mezzanine floor of the new store, 'Woolies' was open for lunch. (*Photographs courtesy of 3D and 6D Pictures Limited*)

Magdalen Street, *c.* 1968. (*Photograph courtesy of Ian Clark at www.ianclarkmusic.com*)

Woolworths had two branches open in 1960s Norwich. Although the Rampant Horse Street branch was big, and extensively modernised, the smaller Magdalen Street branch remained largely unaltered. It is distinguishable here, looking from the corner of Colegate, by the more traditional Woolworths red signage. With its dark wood floors and glass counters, it provided a stark contrast to its sister branch in the city centre.

Popping into 'Woolies' for some pick 'n' mix was always popular, but at the other end of the retail world there was still the small independent shop. The corner shop was once a literal description of these businesses. In the maze of terraced houses, built mainly in the Victorian period, the house on the corner of a street was often slightly larger than the others, and was very often converted into a shop. These were sometimes hairdressers, or greengrocers. Often, they were the sort of shop that sold everything. Occasionally, the shop would also have the post office business as well.

Bishopgate Post Office, mid-1960s. A classic example of the corner shop, doubling up as a post office. You'd be able to post letters, buy stamps and draw your pension here. You'd also be able to pick up a bottle of Corona and some Fruit Salad or Black Jack chews. And of course a packet of Players ... Please. (*Photograph courtesy of Ian Clark at www.ianclarkmusic.com*)

Pottergate, 1960s. (*Photograph courtesy of Ian Clark at www.ianclarkmusic.com*)

Not strictly a corner shop, but Atkins in Pottergate is a glorious example of the little shop that sold everything. The door is covered with advertisements for numerous cigarette and tobacco brands. Brooke Bond and Typhoo Tea are well promoted on the door and window, too. A closer look at the wares on display reveals that here, in the middle of the city, from a very small shop, you could also buy boxes of chocolates, jigsaw puzzles, teddy bears, Birds Eye frozen foods, biscuits, Weetabix and giant tubes of Smarties. That is without the chewing gum available from the machines outside.

There are glimpses into a world that has disappeared in this picture. This was a shop where you could trade in your cigarette coupons, collected with each pack bought and redeemable against more cigarettes or goods in a catalogue. Some of the cigarette brands are long gone. Guards, Cambridge and Cameron at 4s 6d for twenty (22.5p each). No. 6 and Cadets were smaller cigarettes at a lower price.

Among the chocolates there is a box of Reward and of course, Dairy Box. The photograph must have been taken in the run up to Christmas, as the window display also features some sets of glass baubles for the tree, and some selection boxes. The gum machines also display brands from the past. YZ and Wizard bubblegum are there, along with the famous Wrigleys. These machines usually had an added promotion. If the arrow on the handle was pointing forwards when you put your penny in, you got two packs instead of one. In essence, this meant that every fourth customer got double value. It didn't take long before the kids would always check the machine before dropping the coin into the slot.

Nowadays, with mini versions of the big supermarkets in most neighbourhoods, the old corner shop has largely disappeared. Oddly, its ability to sell just about anything now seems less like an old fashioned retail concept and more like the prototype for today's mini-supermarket.

Lower Goat Lane, 1968. Just around the corner from Atkins' shop. The lane typifies the period, and shows some of the concerns raised by the post-war planners. These ancient buildings were now covered by modern signs. In fact, the pub visible at the bottom of the lane, in Pottergate, was specifically mentioned in the 1945 *Plan for Norwich* as having too much signage and too many different typefaces.

There will always be specialist retailers. In 1960s Norwich several shops were, for instance, selling cycles. In 1963, the bike was still a day to day essential for many people, rather than a lifestyle choice. Fieldings, though, were keen to promote a full range of cycles, for all the family. (*Photograph by George Plunkett*)

FIELDINGS

East Anglia's Leading Cycle Agents

'HADDON' CYCLES available only at Fieldings

POPULAR SPORTS TOURISTS
(as illustration)

in two-tone colours.
Single speed models
only ... **£14/17/9**

or fitted with 3-speed
and hub dyno.
only **£19/15/9**

JUVENILE MODELS
16 in. at **£11/19/6**

18 in Sports a 1
Roadsters at **13** Gns

JUNIOR PAVEMENT CYCLES
at **£11/19/6**

LADIES' AND GENT'S ROADSTERS 12 gns.

ALSO IN STOCK THE LATEST 1963 MODELS
RALEIGH, TRIUMPH, B.S.A.

ALL AVAILABLE CASH OR EASY TERMS

Deposits from £1

NORWICH	**LOWESTOFT**
	75 LONDON ROAD
11 PRINCE OF WALES ROAD	**GORLESTON**
	123 and 124 HIGH STREET
24 MAGDALEN STREET	**YARMOUTH**
14 and 16 LOWER GOAT LANE	35 and 36 MARKET ROW

Fieldings, 1963, branches everywhere – and bikes for all the family. Wilmott's, Fieldings and Gale and Galey advertising from 1963 shows just how busy and important a shopping area Prince of Wales Road was at the time. Although still home to dentists, doctors and legal firms, the road was populated with several important retailers.

The teenagers were able to buy, or have bought for them, the Dansette record players and transistor radios, and the whole family could find a bike at Fieldings. Over at Gale and Galey, a very wholesome concept was on display.

Long before the term 'Aga Saga' had entered the language, and quite a while before the brand saw a twenty-first-century surge in middle-class popularity, an Aga was available at Gale and Galey for £130.

The advertising did not concentrate on initial cost, however. It was much more to do with the running costs, which at 15s (75p) a week were attractive even by 1963 standards.

It might have been prudent to promote the Aga on long term economy. £130 for the famous oven seems cheap in the twenty-first century, but compare the price to the Rayburn also on offer. At £72 19s 3d (£72.95), it was only just over half the price of an Aga.

It's running costs that really count!

Modern Cookers

Cost only 15'- to 18'- a week to run

They provide cooking and heating facilities in the most economical way possible.

(on left)

THE AGA (with 5 - year Guarantee)

A luxury cooker which operates by stored heat and controlled heat. Provides perfect cooking constant hot water, roasting oven and simmering oven, and, above all, guaranteed economy.

Price **£130**

(on right) **The RAYBURN ROYAL**

An efficient cooker at reasonable cost, giving
★ Wonderful Cooking   ★ Ample Hot Water
★ Warmth for the whole of your kitchen

FROM **£72/19/3**

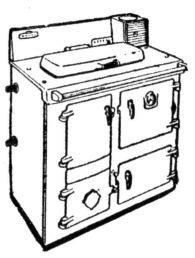

C·U·C

As Members of C.U.C. we can supply either of these appliances on **NO DEPOSIT** terms and payments over 5 years under the N.C.B. scheme

INSTALLATION COST included in deferred terms if required.

Our representative will gladly call and advise you on any heating problem without obligation

GALE & GALEY

75 Prince of Wales Road, Norwich. 22730
Open until 5.30 p.m.

5 Drayton Road, Norwich.   45466
Open until 6 p.m.

Aga and Rayburn from Gale and Galey, 1963.

TOP QUALITY
Used Cars

KING'S (OF NORWICH)

FULLY GUARANTEED
Used Cars

KICK OFF WITH A WINNER—
BUY NOW ONE OF OUR TIP-TOP, QUALITY-TESTED,
FULLY GUARANTEED USED CARS

1961 **FORD CONSUL** Saloon, radio, disc brakes, safety belts, heater, etc., etc., one owner lime green £539
1959 **AUSTIN A35** 2-door de luxe Saloon, green, an excellent example £339
1961 **FORD POPULAR** de luxe Saloon, powder blue, low mileage £369
1961 **MORRIS MINOR** '1000' de luxe 2-door, blue, in lovely condition £419

1959 **AUSTIN HEALEY** Sprite, soft top radio, heater, in white, lovely performance £369
1959 **AUSTIN A35** 4-door de luxe Saloon, in ivory, heater, etc., excellent £329
1960 **MORRIS OXFORD** Ser. V de luxe, white lovely condition £499
1961 **AUSTIN 7 MINI** car, one owner, grey, excellent example £359
1960 **VOLKSWAGEN** de luxe Saloon, coral, one owner, low mileage £489

1961 **RENAULT DAUPHINE** de luxe Saloon, 4 speed, one careful owner, as new £419
1961 **FORD CONSUL** de luxe Saloon, blue a one-owner ultra-clean car £549
1961 **MORRIS MINI MINOR** Saloon, fitted Neros stage 2 head and many modifications, high performance with economy, blue, one owner £429
1957 **MORRIS MINOR** '1000' 2-door de luxe Saloon, black, superb car £319

Cut Out This Coupon and Post Today

I am interested in a King's Guaranteed Used Car, in the price range marked with " X "
£150-£250 ☐   £250-£350 ☐
£350-£500 ☐   Over £500 ☐
I have for Part Exchange a 19......
year make.......... model........
for which I expect £..............
NAME ....
ADDRESS ....
....
....

PART EXCHANGES WELCOMED . . .
. . . LOWEST POSSIBLE DEPOSITS

ALL CARS SOLD WITH KING'S WRITTEN GUARANTEE
And don't forget **KING'S ACTUALLY PAY YOUR INSTAL-MENTS FOR YOU** in the event of **SICKNESS, ACCIDENT** or **UNEMPLOYMENT**

NO BETTER TERMS AVAILABLE ANYWHERE—CALL TODAY—DRIVE AWAY
9 a.m.-6 p.m., Thursday 1 p.m.

2 SPROWSTON ROAD, NORWICH
TELEPHONE 45225

Car bargains at Kings, 1963.

As your lifestyle improved in the better years of the 1960s, you were probably considering the purchase of a car. This was, as it still is, an important financial decision. First cars were often second hand, and this glimpse into the Kings of Norwich used car listings from 1963 gives us come context of the costs.

The advertisement has a neat marketing technique in place, whereby you sent back the coupon to say which price range you were interested in, so they could obtain your name and address. Today it is called data capture. The lowest price bracket starting at £150 is only £20 more expensive than an Aga. However, a second hand car at £150 in 1963 was costing roughly the equivalent of six weeks' wages, before any deductions.

A 1961 Renault Dauphine, heavily advertised on TV at the time, could be yours for £419. Meanwhile, a 1959 Austin Healey Sprite was a relative bargain at £369. Which one would be worth more today?

This year hire a self-drive caravan from us and go where you want – when you want!

4-BERTH CARAVETTE

Our terms are the most reasonable in East Anglia. Comprehensively insured.

Fully-equipped 4-Berth Caravettes.

Also **Hillman Minx** and **Vauxhall Self-drive Cars on highly competitive terms.**

TUCKSWOOD SERVICE STATION

HALL ROAD, NORWICH   Telephone 26016

The Caravette, 1967: go where you want, when you want.

Sherries beyond compare

DOMECQ'S

MAGNOLA
Fino

THE PERFECT APERITIF
AND THE

Irresistible NORWICH CREAM

A RARE OLD OLOROSO OF GREAT AGE

Sole Distributors BARWELL & SONS · NORWICH

Barwell's, 1961. There were no more specialist retailers than Barwell's. The long-established local wine merchants were able to sell the 'irresistable' Norwich Cream, a sherry named after the city. It was available on draught.

The 1960s were also the time when more and more families contemplated holidays. Although the overseas package tour was becoming fashionable, the UK market was still strong. For those who wanted to travel around at home, but had not yet reached the dizzy height of car ownership, there was the idea of hiring a vehicle.

In 1967, the Caravette had not attained the hippy status it would later acquire. This was a 1960s attempt to create a competitor to the touring caravan.

This early 1960s advertisement for the East Anglian Trustees Savings Bank, with its promise of a £94 return on £500 invested for seven years, is interesting. Starting off with a positive message, it points out that there are benefits over and above the purely financial. Ease of withdrawal for instance makes the EATB a convenient place. There are no charges, except for standing orders. Then, with an eerie resonance given the bail-outs of the twenty-first century, it proclaims that there is 'Safety – Guaranteed by the Government'.

Their fourth point – 'There are no worries with Trustees Savings Bank Accounts' – does sound like a rather general one, as if the advertisement is running out of steam.

The origins of the East Anglian Trustees Savings Bank are not dissimilar to those of a corner shop. The bank had begun life when, in 1812, John Cole had set up a 'bank' in his own house in Norwich. It gained customers from the working classes, and in particular apprentices. These 'industrious poor' were worthy of some security and a board of trustees was set up to run the rapidly expanding bank. As it developed and opened branches in other places, including Great Yarmouth, the East Anglian Trustees Saving Bank was formed. Legislation in the 1970s altered the Trustees Savings Banks and within a few more years, the entire network had become part of what we now know as Lloyds TSB.

Insure here with the NORWICH UNION INSURANCE GROUP FOR SERVICE AND SECURITY

£500 TODAY

£594 . 5 . 0

in 7 years

ORDINARY DEPARTMENT
UP TO
£15 Per Year INTEREST
FREE OF INCOME TAX

There are other considerations as well as Rates of Interest when investing . . .

1 Ease of Deposit and Withdrawal

2 Except for Standing Orders — No Bank Charges

3 Safety — Guaranteed by the Government

4 There are no worries with Trustee Savings Bank Accounts

EAST ANGLIAN TRUSTEE SAVINGS BANK

Branches Throughout East Anglia

Although Norwich was still very much a manufacturing city in the 1960s, the finance sector was a vital part of the local economy. Norwich Union, in its pre-Aviva days, was a big employer. Its branding at the time was almost understated given its size. Two financial institutions with a decidedly local background were the East Anglian Trustees Savings Bank and the Norwich Building Society.

Safeguard Your Interest

For ease of mind today and independence in the future invest **NOW** in the Norwich Building Society.

Every penny invested is secured by assets exceeding £12,000,000, and backed by more than a century of service to the public.

Full details of how **your** *money can earn a steady profit are available free on request to the address below.*

Invest in the

  **BUILDING SOCIETY**

ST. ANDREW'S HOUSE · NORWICH · TELEPHONE 21367

TOTAL ASSETS EXCEED £12,000,000

DEPOSITS IN THIS SOCIETY ARE TRUSTEE INVESTMENTS

The Norwich Building Society would merge to become the Norwich and Peterborough Building Society in 1986. In the 1960s, it was still in its original guise. It is a significantly different approach from today's marketing, as the total assets of the company are clearly stated in the advertising. For details of how your money can earn a 'steady' profit, it's up to you to write for details.

Working in a building society, bank, or any office during the 1960s was rather different to twenty-first-century office life. By far and away most people smoked, and it was perfectly acceptable to do so at work. The atmosphere was often dense with cigarette smoke, and it was noisier, too. In an email and computer keyboard world, today's offices are virtually silent by comparison. In a 1960s office the telephones rang, loudly, all the time. Often there were two telephones on someone's desk, one for external calls, the other for internal. The networks were separate. They all rang with loud bells and buzzers, and everybody was talking on them, which meant the volume went up to make oneself heard.

Over and above the telephone bells and voices, there was the clattering of typewriter. Electric typewriters arrived during the 1960s. They were expensive, and it was impractical to replace all of a company's manual machines in one go anyway. So, although they were a little quieter, they were not instantly numerous enough to make a difference to the overall volume level of the office.

Norwich Typewriters Limited

DISTRIBUTORS OF . . .

ROYAL TYPEWRITERS

Electric, Standard and Portable
for the County of Norfolk

TYPEWRITERS

Office Equipment Specialists

55 PRINCE OF WALES ROAD · NORWICH
Telephone Norwich 22714

Norwich Typewriters Limited, 1961. Everything the modern office needed, available on Prince of Wales Road.

The arrival of computers would change office life forever. Everybody became a typist, not a skilled typist in the way that generations of secretaries had been, but a typist of necessity, able to tap out emails and documents on their own keyboard. Email removed the need for countless telephone calls and reduced the noise.

Where the computer and digital revolution changed office life beyond recognition, though, was in the world of graphic design and advertising. Well into the 1960s and beyond, all design work was carried out with a pencil or magic marker. Drawing boards were the order of the day, and in advertising agency studios the relatively recent innovation of Letraset had been the biggest technology change for years. This 'rub-down' lettering system meant that the skilled, but time consuming, practice of hand lettering for designs was no longer needed. By the time the computer arrived, that massive advance seemed like an ancient art. Cigarette smoke aside the studios smelled of Cow Gum. This rubber solution was the adhesive of choice for designers to glue together the artwork they prepared for press advertisements, packaging designs, posters and leaflets.

Photocopying was not a simple job, and often involved wet and dry rollers to 'fix' the copy. The fax was still science fiction, but messages could be sent by the telex system. All but forgotten now, the telex was something that companies embraced as new technology, proudly displaying their telex number in the way a company would publicise their website address today.

It involved typing messages into strips of punch tape, which were then fed through the machine to transmit them through the telephone system. There was one major problem that caused much confusion: you could only type a telex message in capitals, as the keyboard had no lower case.

The studio at Tibbenham Advertising, 1967. Tibbenhams was the major advertising agency in Norwich in the 1960s. This picture of the design and production studio shows the drawing boards, glue pots, draughtsman's instruments and filing cabinets that would become obsolete as computer-driven design became the norm.

Interestingly, in this room there are no telephones visible. Not everybody was considered sufficiently senior to have their own telephone extension. A central one, on the desk of the boss, was the means of communicating with the artists.

Offices in the 1960s, exactly like the Tibbenham's studio, were not places to have your lunch. In the twenty-first century, the working day has become much more flexible, and people tend to eat at their desks.

If you were to walk into an office at lunchtime in the 1960s, it was usually empty, because people went out to eat. Some, of course, doubtless went for the business lunch that was so much part of the culture. The pub was also a much more popular, and accepted, part of lunchtime culture.

Tastes were changing and many establishments were trying new cuisine. Some of the cafés had disappeared. The Kosy Korner, for instance, had gone as part of the Queens Road alterations.

There was still plenty of choice. Here's a glimpse back at some of the places open for business in 1960s Norwich.

THE

BOAR'S HEAD

CONTINENTAL RESTAURANT
AND THREE
FULLY LICENSED BARS

BE

SURE

TO

VISIT

St. Stephen's • Norwich

(Opposite Marks & Spencers)

Open for Lunch from 11 a.m.–2.30 p.m.

Dinner from 5.30 p.m.–Midnight

RESTAURANT FULLY LICENSED UNTIL 11.30 p.m.

The Boar's Head. Proudly locating itself as 'opposite Marks and Spencers', this was a large establishment in St Stephens. Note the intriguing reference to a 'Continental Restaurant'.

VISITORS TO NORWICH
Come to
VALORI'S RESTAURANT
(Timber Hill)

FAMOUS FOR ITS FISH AND CHIPS
Open from 11 a.m. to 11.30 p.m.

Valoris, a map to make sure you found them. They had several branches including the one in Rose Lane where The Beatles dined after their show in 1963.

NORFOLK RAILWAY HOUSE

PRINCE OF WALES ROAD, NORWICH

(Opposite Thorpe Station)

Commencing

Monday, April 1st

We shall be serving in the

BAMBOO ROOM

Grills, Luncheons

Snacks

11.30 a.m.-2 p.m.

BULLARDS BEERS

The Norfolk Railway House. Again, specific location details (Opposite Thorpe Station) and another intriguing reference to a particular style. This time it's the 'Bamboo Room'. Locally brewed Bullards beers are proudly mentioned.

The Cloverleaf. This time we're 'Off Market Place'. Straightforward advertising, offering good food at moderate prices.

Whilst in Norwich

VISIT

STANNARDS

COFFEE HOUSE AND
LICENSED RESTAURANT

GRILLS, CHICKEN DISHES
OMELETTES

Menu available all day until 10.15 p.m.

ALL SAINTS GREEN
NORWICH

Above: A famous Norwich name, Stannards. They had more than one café, which by the 1960s were called coffee houses.

Opposite: Lanchow on Prince of Wales Road. Chinese restaurants 1960s style. The two-person dinner cost 18/- (90p) and included tea and coffee. For 38/-, a party of four could eat. That's 45p each!

LANCHOW CHINESE RESTAURANT

22 PRINCE OF WALES ROAD NORWICH
(Fully Licensed)

Some Special Menus Recommended by the Management

DINNER

FOR 2 PERSONS 18/-

Mushroom and Chicken Soup
Fried Sweet and Sour Pork
Stewed Pineapple with Chicken
Special Fried Rice

FOR 3 PERSONS 26/-

Chop Suey Soup with Noodle
Fried Lobster Balls
Fried Sweet and Sour Pork
Fried Chicken with Mixed Vegetables
Beef Chop Suey
Plain Fried Rice

FOR 4 PERSONS 32/-

Meat Ham and Bamboo Shoot Soup
Fried Lobster with Mixed Vegetables
Stewed Chicken with White Mushroom
Chinese Roast Pork with Greens
Chinese Omelette and Special Fried Rice

FOR 4 PERSONS 38/-

Noodle Soup with Chicken
Fried Sweet and Sour Lobster Balls
Stewed Chicken Almond with Bamboo Shoot
Special Chinese Roast Chicken
Special Fried Rice and Fried Prawns in Sauce

TEA OR COFFEE INCLUSIVE

County Hall of Martineau Lane, under construction at a cost of £2.5 million, 1967. As the 1960s were drawing to a close, two more significant buildings were built: one on the edge of the city, the other in the centre. (*Photographs by George Plunkett*)

Her Majesty's Stationery Office, Anglia Square. Her Majesty's Stationery Office is the organisation that publishes all the government's legislative papers on behalf of the Queen. It is an enormous function and includes the printing of the records of parliamentary proceedings known throughout the world as Hansard. They are verbatim records and some of the most important archives in politics. (*Photograph by George Plunkett*)

County Hall was built in 1967 and opened by Her Majesty Queen Elizabeth II on 24 May 1968. The architect was Reginal Uren. His bold, modern design caused some discussion. There was no doubt that the building was needed. Changes in political structure meant that the County Council's workload had dramatically increased since the 1950s.

In 1969, another major new building was opened in the city centre. In the Anglia Square district, which had emerged from the changes around Magdalen Street, Her Majesty's Stationery Office opened impressive new premises.

Near to the offices of HMSO is a small lane, called Hansard Lane. It is a small tribute to Luke Hansard, the printer who gave his name to the records. It is fitting that this huge operation was to be placed in Anglia Square. The building is in the Parish of St Mary's. It was there, in Norwich, in 1752, that Luke Hansard, perhaps one of the most famous printers of all, was born and apprenticed. His great enterprise had come home to Norwich in the 1960s.

ALSO BY PETE GOODRUM

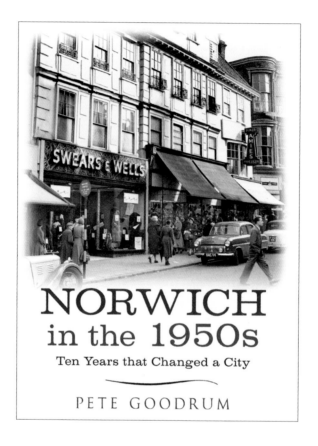

Norwich in 1950 was a different place. Still scarred by war, the city was coming to terms with itself. Children played in the rubble of bomb sites, and workers strove to build a prosperous peace on building sites.

By the end of the decade, the retail heart of the city would be reconstructed, new building programmes would be changing domestic life and the manufacturing industries would be making world-class products with household names.

Birthplace of Barclays, Aviva, Start-Rite and Colmans, the city was ready to embark on another chapter in its long history of commercial and cultural development.

From post-war austerity to the threshold of the consumer society, Norwich embraced the 1950s as a decade of change.

Pete Goodrum's bestselling book gives a fascinating insight to the decade before the 1960s.

978 1 4456 0906 5
96 pages, full colour